MW01286752

Stone Fruit

Stephen Yenser

WAYWISER

First published in 2016 by

THE WAYWISER PRESS

Christmas Cottage, Church Enstone, Chipping Norton, Oxfordshire, OX7 4NN, UK
P.O. Box 6205, Baltimore, MD 21206, USA
http://waywiser-press.com

Editor-in-Chief
Philip Hoy

Senior American Editor
Joseph Harrison

Associate Editors
Eric McHenry | Dora Malech | V. Penelope Pelizzon | Clive Watkins
Greg Williamson | Matthew Yorke

9 7 5 3 1 2 4 6 8

A CIP catalogue record for this book is available from the British Library

ISBN 978-1-904130-81-9

Printed and bound by
T. J. International Ltd., Padstow, Cornwall, PL28 8RW

To Melissa and Helen
and in memory of James Merrill

Acknowledgments

Burnside Review: Prospect, Codicil

Dublin Poetry Review: The Relic

Fulcrum: An Anthology of Poetry and Poetics: Autumnal (Hölderlin), Old Man in a Waterfront Taverna, Little Fundamentalist Song

Great River Review: Three Self-Portraits: The Last Judgment (Detail), The Broken Column, St. Jerome in the Desert

Horace: *The Odes*: Wealth (Horace): Odes 2.17, Odes 3.16, Odes 3.24

Northwest Review: The Amherst Daguerreotype [as Brace for Barbara], The Eel (Montale)

Poem-a-Day: Academy of American Poets: Santorini

Poetry: *Hija* on Emerson's Birthday, Musing, Preserves, Psalm on Sifnos, Wichita Triptych

Slate: Variations for Three Old Saws

Southwest Review: Akbar

The Antioch Review: Post-Avant Pastoral

Volt: Catullan Canticles: To Lucy, For Muse, Her Parakeet

Yale Review: Desk: An Address, Cycladic Idyll: An Apologia

CONTENTS

I

II

III

IV

CONTENTS

I

Prospect

So there you'll be, burro dead long ago,
Lost as the map, with no directions to follow

Except those of deranged Joshua trees,
And rootless, extravagant as tumbleweed,

Desiccated, seedy, seed yet to spill
Withal, but nothing left to wet your whistle,

Let alone whet it, as the dark falls sharply,
Winds rise to keen in a minor key,

And your illuminated Book of Matches
Flares up sulfur-scented, while your watch's

Time runs out into the sand beneath
Your feet. It leaves with your words to eat.

Cycladic Idyll: An Apologia

"I don't know why you don't just go over to Catalina."
—William Edinger

1

I come here for the views.

I come because there is no news.

Because things have been arranged. Because I have no other
plans. Because there are no plans for me. Because I do
not have to choose.

I come here for the arid, aromatic, aromantic emptiness—where
one might "get a grip" and "sort things out." Add them
up. Make some sum. Compose oneself—like a concerto
for flute and strings.

I come to be alone. Because I am alone. Out of season. Like the
few midges left. Adrift on a stony island no known poet
hails from. Enisled. Outlandish as that term. (*Annihiled* is
different but only by a smidge.)

To remind myself how simple things can be. Simple as the music
of the marble figures of the harpist—and the unique
double-reed player.

Not to mention concepts. To remind myself how when it comes
to things like concepts, Heraclitus and Plato had all we
would ever need. (Pythagoras I set aside for now.)

I come here to learn to speak clearly. To make carefully with the
right mouthparts the sounds for *thing* and *nothing*, for
bread and *wine*, for *come* and *go*, *here* and *now* and *then*
and *there*. For *good evening* and *farewell*.

Because my own language has become extravagant and tra-la,
      tra-la. Tralatitious, one might say. And—the olives every-
      where remind me—indecently indehiscent.

Because I want fewer such words to weigh. To be less weighword,
      so to say. Therefore less wayward and less spendthrift.
      Less spindrift, in a word.

Not to mention grave, preponderant, and dark. (I come here to be
      struck by *lightening*!)

Because here in the right place a *thésis* can be a good flat stone
      to sit on and not a lizardlike thing to nail down then
      argue with.

Because here amid abandoned villages' abundant dilapidation
      there is no reason for reason, no urge to originality.

Because as I wait to be transported I read on small trucks that ply
      the main road the descriptor *Metaphorá*.

I come here to sit at length and read some Whitman, who adored
      words plain as stones, regardless of those exultant
      exaltations of "eidolons."

To browse idly, to idle on in a brief, worn lexicon, to let it lead
      me on.

Because I need new old sayings. Because the good ones die too
      soon. Because bean by bean fills the bag.

Because I will save time, because it will not save me, here where
      it twists on itself like the walkways to waylay laid-up
      freebooters like me and my dead friend.

2

I come back to stop in on the way to see this time by appointment
    Edward Lear's watercolors in the Gennadius,

Because he did them as sketches for oils he could paint then
    sell back home, so they were valueless themselves, so
    they were kept unmatted and loose in cartons pulled off
    shelves thirty years ago for improvident visitors like me
    and my friend who was my guide to shuffle through and
    take quick notes like these on his.

Because even this delicate, vehicular medium meant fixity, his
    nemesis, so in hopes that glazed and scumbled oils
    could get the shifty shades right, he jotted in light pencil
    across the images descriptions, shot through with nonce
    terms and puns fleeting as pains taken, rubbed and
    faded, sometimes indecipherable, wishful notes written
    on washes disappearing before our eyes, which follow
    them, into sea, cliff, olive stand, distant temple, dovecote,
    asphodel.

"catch gold light grass" "all turquoisy & Byzantine bluesy" "O
    poppies!" "very olivish"

3

I come here not to contemn my city's columbaria of
        condominiums and book emporia with their stacks of
        fresh books on chocolate chockablock with guides to the
        Galapagos and *Godot* and their tables laden with books
        on coffee tables and books on coffee table books,

And not to malign the midnight supermarkets' own tropic
        aisles, with their tanned and juicy, shrink-wrapped
        dates, their bruise-ripe figs burnished by gelled lights
        (O psychedelicacies!) and the racks of razors and glossy
        magazines and analgesics.

I come not to ditch the academy's deliciously multiplicitous
        pharmakon, though disembarking I accidentally dropped
        into the sea my faithful Dopp kit, full of the life-saving
        medicines that took it down, perhaps as it chose, since it
        seemed to leap from my hand through an opening just its
        size.

I come here to address not deconstruction but myself.

To address myself to the oregano (a whiff on the breeze nostalgic
        and heady as skunk) cropping up beside the ubiquitous
        retaining walls and boundary walls,

Built of the ubiquitous stone, culled from the fields, or axed
        and levered out of outcrops, sometimes faced or split,
        sometimes filled with scrabbled up rubble, fitted,
        mortarless, tight as puzzle pieces,

Built with what would now be tortuous lifting, hugging, and
        lugging, done under the long, low sun over decades,
        decades of decades, the stones settling in subtly, row on row,

Adamant and indistinct as the years themselves, by hard men
      faceless and various as the stones themselves.

According to lore, the discontented among them come back at
      night during autumn to fields pitch dark beneath the vast
      broadcast of stars

To monitor their work, to make repairs to those boundaries that
      are their bonds with this world.

Each has many, many headstones, none with a name.

They did not (O, onanistic onomastician!) make names for
      themselves, those men,

But wallstones, and courses of them, since stone by stone makes
      a wall, and walls make farming, and farming, homes.

Homes they went back to at dusk and maybe beat their women
      in, in the unbeatable heat, and maybe had hard or fearful
      sex in, as the parching *meltémi* lashed the night and the
      fishermen's lashed-up boats apart,

And anyway yelled things they sometimes did not think could be
      set down in words,

Who set these stones they harvested in place for all but ever.

4

I come because, above the oldest bases of the walls, hunks of
strata large enough one sees why Titans needed to be
conjured,

A former Roman Catholic church contains in three small rooms
remains of a treasury, which is a *thesaurús*, which is also
why I come,

And a marble fragment one could hold in one hand like a bunch
of grapes, itself a treasure, a clutch of breasts from a copy
of the Ephesian goddess (herself a copy of a wooden
effigy decked with strings of tear-shaped amber beads),

And several "parting scenes," the people in chitons and hima-
tions, from funerary sculptures.

I come to find these smaller puzzles and pieces of puzzles and to
find the small peace that lies in that.

To find the only bougainvillea I have ever seen that has been
trimmed and pleached to look like a tree, until you get
up close and see that it entwines itself like time itself in a
kind of solo orgy,

And then remind yourself of what he wrote, that *truth* shoots out
from the same root as *tree* not because it is steadfast but
because it may be pruned and keeps branching—

To which I add it soaks up light and turns it into shade, is shady,
makes a place for *trysts*, a place one *trusts*, as long as
one's not spooked by other shades, of *druids* and
hamadryads, who hang out there, like invisible fruit,
swelling, ripe, windfallen, wizened.

To sip each evening's ouzo, which is truly mother's milk when ice
is added (as he, smiling, would understand).

To loaf and invite the soul and discover anew rabbit stew and be
ridiculously pleased that it is an item in a *katálogos*,

And once a week religiously to gorge on retsina and goat (ah,
efcharistó is exactly what we must say, he could have
said), so tough on the hillside in the crucifying sun and so
forgivingly tender after three days in the pot.

I come because from its peak this island with its bights
and spits is a puzzle piece among others in the
archipelago, mountains up to their necks in blue-green
solitude.

5

I come back here to rough it, to rough it out, to draft, to draw. To
withdraw—and to *vise* my self, as they once said, and to
revise, or let it stand and deliver. Make it stand and
confess. Out of chagrin. And in embarrassment. Out of
shame. And in humiliation.

I come back here with my notebook and the amber kombolöi
he gave me like a least rosary of 33 beads to tell, to say
mín ksechnáte, carefully, over and over, alone on a path
outside one of the 365 "churches" the guide book assures
me—without elucidation—are here, because at home,
indelibly and in public, I forgot how to say *don't forget*.

To remember for instance that while our word *fast* runs from and
to itself, and the word pronounced *akrivós* cleaves
instantly, *permanent* and *quick* overlap like small waves,
as do *accurate* and *expensive*, and anyway they are all
one word if we could spell.

To find not that word but sherds of it here and there, as in
petróchorto, or *stonecrop*, ancient remedy and poison.
Stonecrop.

(And then to recall that *kápou-kápou* means at once *now and
then* and *here and there* and feel for a moment I might be
getting warmer.)

To walk out in search of a shaft of the fabulous and flooded mines
and come across a sarcophagus that is the goats' water
trough.

To pick one fieldstone up and bang it with a larger one into a
chink in the terrace wall beneath the kastro, from which

one can see the other islands' eidolons afloat in the
in-between—ultramarine—ultramundane—Plato's *tó
metaxí*—anyone's and no one's,

And where someone, no one now, built long ago flush into
the wall where the steep path turns firmly as a verse
enjambed an ancient basin—unobtrusive as a fit quote—
its marble weathering to rock again, and someone
installed above it a modern spigot. And then removed the
handle.

6

I come back to learn the Greek for *handle*.

To find by the way the Scrabble trove *parémia* meant first a
thing discovered either "by the route" or "by the song,"
something used and left by those who went before.

To saunter for a jaunty moment along the quay, to wonder at the
water, to see that the sea's ceaselessness makes the proto-
watercolor, the Idea of watercolor.

To think that while naming shades—of lipstick, say—might be
a gratifying occupation, and perhaps profession, that is
another matter entirely—and even possible.

To confirm that each year more fish slip away and leave their
shed tints wriggling in the shoals like hints of souls.

To discover that nothing changes. Or only nothing does. Changes
everything. Always has done, will do. Will have to do,
here at the end of the day.

It soughs, it saws softly in the surrounding, redundant *hush*, blue
as blue, blue of the first water, yet clear in the palms'
overflowing cup as *tsípouro*. (*Tsípouro*: a spirit condensed
from residue, from *must*.)

I come back thinking to come upon something he might like,
moving but dry, moving, yet cold and still, like these
shallows, profoundly transparent,

And I am in over my head again, where it all flows, beginning with
the simplest language, where once some tongue-slip led to
slime then slid along to *loam* and *lime* and then *oblivion*,

23

While even stone is hardly faster, sea creatures secreting shells
    whose limestone pressed to marble harbors streaming
    linen.

I come back because I cannot stay away. Because I cannot stay.
    Because I must.

I come back to leave. Not to leave a mark, either. To take it,
    rather. Like a vow. A vow of silence, say.

Or just a *volta*, the evening turn along the littoral that turns
    imaginal beneath my feet. To take it and to leave it, then.
    To leave my take—as pirates and directors have it—and to
    take my leave away.

Wichita Triptych

Sometimes the rain shines
Just when the sun reigns,
And that is the way it was
Since that was the way it is
Beyond the French doors
That late afternoon here
In this mind's early evening
Where they still fade in
That cool color Polaroid,
Pastels of her prom dress,
Its bowl of double peonies,
Promising, precocious,
Trying, trying to open.

*

Wichita Triptych

Their friend and he were tight
Tight-rope walkers, self-taught
Taut-trope-talkers, stalking
Jamb-up, arm-in-arm
And caroling to lucky stars
Of cars, bars, and rebar,
The night a carousel
Of smoky tryst and troth,
Of casual carousals,
Cocky arousals,
Pitching the dark to the dark.
(Streetlight and moth,
Reader, she married both.)

*

But then there he was,
In the morning's mourning,
Soi-disant
Proustian mignon,
Aesthetic ascetic
And Kansas rube
Reducing his thought
To a bouillon cube
No one suitably hot
Ought ever pore over.

Preserves

Nervy, sparrow-like,
Eyes Cherokee,
Blackberry black,
Arrow-quick,
Picky eater,
Meager spirit,
Converted Quaker,
She taught her grandson
Arithmetic
And pruning tactics
And let him touch
Through her cotton nightie
Small, tense nipples.
Her hands, arthritic,
Knitted doilies,
Breaded tomatoes,
Puréed apples,
And put up apricots,
While the hoarded guilts
Made for bright quilts,
The torrid migraines'
Counterpanes.

The Relic

Library vault unlocked,
our friend the curator picks out a casket
that opens brashly on the lock
of hair: a curl of bright auburn
("bold, like the Chestnut Burr,"
she'd offered, turning inner
outer, merging husk and kernel,
a banked fire burning).
An urgent yearning, an awful favor
rises … I'm dying to ask it.

The Amherst Daguerreotype

Barbara Packer (1947-2010)

1. "And a Torrid Eye"

A demimondaine's
Demand—

Kohl-dark, jet-dark—
Or look of Jeanne d'Arc—

The koh-i-noor's
Start—or a black

Diamond's heart—
A star diamond

Mine's depth—
Deep as her mind's

Own word-hoard mined
For half-whored words—

Adored—redeemed—
By whom she deemed

All but damned.

2. "Could mortal lip divine"

Sheens of a suit
Shiny from funerals—

Suit pressed and repressed—
Proved and reproved—

Colors of dolor
Unsung—yet sung—

Hersed and rehearsed—
Black mail—

Funest armor
Warding, rewording ardor—

Rustless—restless—
Full of nought—but null—

Ah, darkness—her muse—
Your muse—her darkness—

Your perfect—pitch.

Three Self-Portraits

1. The Last Judgment (Detail)

Some hack's belated drapery
cannot emasculate the saint
who looks up like a gladiator

triumphant for the sign from God-
the-Man (whose muscled contrapposto
fulgidly overshadows his)

and flashes the honed flensing blade
in his right hand and grips in his left
the pelt of Michelangelo

(lugubrious scowl on the dark face,
the rest limp as a wet chamois),
serving his own hard sentence,

whose bristle brush hued from washes
of thinned pigment exuding light
thewy Bartholomew's bare thighs.

2. The Broken Column

The fractured col-
umn's strapped fast
whose capital
like a balled fist
upholds the almost
beheaded Kahlo's
chin while the down
around her mouth
makes a young Christ
nailed to the board
and her spiled eyes
that shed petals
of milk-white tears
hold ours as hard
as her nipples above
which forever hovers,
brow-wings
impartible
as pain and paint,
her constant condor.

3. St. Jerome in the Desert

Roughly blocked, mane brushed
brusquely out, the ochre lion

howls the need his healer knows,
whose tanned skin tightens to bone

it's stretched upon (tauter than
that new sailcloth on strainers, taut

as in the anorexic's dream),
in this proof in the *paragone*

where Leonardo's oil turns stone
his painstakingly underpainted

saint, face anguish-lit, his man
in the moon reflecting radiance

bathing the background den
(the lion's—soon Jerome's tomb,

wall etched with a crucifix), his own
forsaken self who to atone

pounds his flesh with rock till one
of them turn fine as pigment ground

for work that he may not abandon,
the work that he cannot see done.

II

Autumnal (Hölderlin)

1. Harvest Time

Wolfgang Nehring (1939-2013)

Ripe, plunged in fire, the fruits
Are cooked and proved upon the earth, and it's a law
That everything goes in, serpentine,
Oracular, dreaming on
The hills of heaven. And much
Like a load of logs
Across the shoulders must
Be salvaged. But the trails
Are treacherous. Unreined, that is,
Like horses, the fixed
Principles and ancient
Laws of the earth run free. And longing
Always ends in endlessness. Much, however, must
Be salvaged. And faith is fate.
Forward, however, and backward, we will
Not look. Let us be lulled, as
By the rowboat's rocking on the lake.

2. Midlife

Laden with yellow pears
And wild roses,
The land lolls in the lake,
And drunk with kisses,
You lovely swans,
You dunk your heads
In sobering holy water.

Ah, where will I find, when
Winter comes, blossoms, and where
Sunshine
And earthly shadows?
The walls stand
Speechless and cold and in the wind
Weathercocks clatter.

Desk: An Address

And broghte him sauf upon a table
Which to the lond him hath upbore.

Gower, *Confessio Amantis, VIII*

1

Well, then, I guess not "desk" as much as "table,"
If one has old romance in mind (again).
And this one's true: "true as a tree," we'd said
In Kansas. It's steady, firm, dependable,
This partner that's supported one for—what?—
These last four decades now and more of drifting,
If not like Apollonius shipwrecked …
It's what one rides on—*writes* on, that is—daily,
Or nightly, if too often weakly—*weekly*,
I mean. But worth the writing *on*? Surely not.

Though in one's ideal study it would be
A writing desk, a secretary, crafted
Like a Chinese treasure box of quartersawn
Sapele, fragrant still when rubbed till warm,
With drop-dead grain, and tiers of cubbyholes,
A drop-down desk, blind doors, dovetailed drawers,
Compartments hidden—a repository
For *secrets*, in a word. Indeed, a kind
Of wooden analogue of that word's warren
Of associations: a place for items
That need to be *secluded* and *secure*,
Related to *seduction* and *sedition*—
And *self* itself in several antic guises.

2

When you lay dying in bucolic Kansas
(And "learning how to make this next transition"),
I sat here in Los Angeles, dying,
How much more slowly, to get "your poem" right,
The dictionary (a faithful "tonic diary,"
Our quick friend quipped, who knew my weaknesses
Inside out) spread open on this desk—
Plunderable and pale as you, it struck me,
In that moonwashed wheatfield near Wichita,
My elbow awkward, painful
On ground and grain an awkward elbow lamp
Lights up again where I reworked the words
Lying here on a finish ruined long
Before (like that of many of the poems—
Well, all of them—at least those far enough
Along to be thought of as "well-begun").

The dictionary told me *desk* connects
Quaintly with *discus*, tool used, as in a harrow,
To till the soil. (Ah, I could see you wince
Less from the figure than the "scholarship"—
Itself now derelict, a grounded vessel.)
And *disk*, from Greek *dikein*, to throw, stems
From Indo-European *deik-*, to show,
Also to speak out frankly, solemnly,
As though to show and tell were still one thing,
As certainly they must have been in Eden,
Before contrariness, old ouroboros,
Could disengage its head and make a tale.
See also *dictionary* proper—and *addict*
(Since we were both ones, so to speak, to "art,"
While *ar-* meant something like "to fit together"),

Edict through *maledict* and on to *verdict*,
From *dedication* to *Eurydike*.

I thought I'd bring you back from France (or Hell),
Where we had gone to write and paint, to tell
And show, as though we were in truth a unit,
Not from the start mismatched catastrophes.
But one day when I turned around you'd gone
From our hill town into the Pyrenees
To unearth meanings of the Black Madonna.

3

Our rustic rental featured *"un grand bureau
Antique."* But this is just a desk. Some plain
Pine planks—plain as your Great Plains soft wood coffin—
One simple-minded yet divided drawer,
Contents packed tight: calculator, ruler,
Magnifying glass from the OED
Now boxed up out of reach above the computer,
A superannuated address book
(Listing your second husband and your children),
Staple extractor, rubber stamps still used
Too often, and a few scored, time-worn tablets
(Little tables!), binder clips, erasers.
Its hardwood legs—maple, with memories
Of sappy youth? or ash, omens of
A fiery end thus far escaped?—have staunchly
Borne up my own to help me get to texts
So dearly purchased, once prized reference volumes,
The "blue book," the bulb blown blind, the nomad spider
Camped in a corner of the desert ceiling.

O *copain* of my pains, O beast of burden,
Animal cheap and charred by cigarettes,
Scarred with *culaccini* from those sweating
Libations, cold and hot, from all those wounds,
Like those bestowed by anyone's long lover,
Gouges and pits filled up with Plastic Wood,
My palimpsest by now of sundry scrapes,
The traces of the daily logodaedaly
And catalogues of errands, and errancies,
Unreadable in its stratigraphy,
Sanded down several times and stained,
(And polished, if never "burnished to its grain")—
First with tung oil (remember our delight?

"OK—*that* love poem writes itself"),
Later Restore-a-Finish—which osmosed
Into drafts before I knew I couldn't
Write on such surfaces and not soak up
A luster that turned into ugly smutch.

4

In turn, it's soaked me up. For all these years
It has absorbed me, luster in my dull ways,
My coffee, ink, and drool, palm sweat, some blood,
And lubricants from tears to Talisker,
Ever since that day you saw it poised,
An Iphigenia ("the strong-born one")
High on a balcony above the alley
In back of an apartment being cleared
For renovation in our college town,
And shouted "Wait! Please! Wait!" The workmen paused—
Verweile doch!—and although nothing waits,
They liked your looks, your *ginger*, and gingerly
Walked it down the stairs, and waited there
Till we could cart it off to our apartment.

5

There is but one, truly serious
Philosophical problem … How we had argued
Camus's notorious thesis! When we broke up,
A sailboat off the coast in the mistral,
Broken in half, the mainsail snapped, prow splintered,
(Who knows what lies there, lost as *lagan* itself),
You salvaged *The Myth of Sisyphus* (in English
Translation, a water-stained paperback).

Later, when given your defining task,
You would not take the treatments they laid down,
The stern mainstream physicians: radiation,
Chemotherapy, tamoxifen
(You'd heard that it would stifle erotic impulse,
The Goddess's). Mastectomy never.
Your days those final weeks were folksy patchworks,
Home remedies and some holistic nostrums:
Juice fasts, concoctions of cayenne and water,
Organic herbal teas, and maple syrup.
A kind of suicide? Refusals of
Refusals to give in prescribed by science.

But first, when you had gone off to become
An "independent person," feminist
And shaman ("shawoman," our quick friend amended),
The long initiation would involve
Peyote and hashish. Yet at the end,
You resisted morphine, because it would
Have severed you from pain, the tough birth cord
Joining us with Mother Earth. "Give us
This day our *pain quotidien*"—or so
It later came to me we could have prayed.

6

One posted photo shows you trying to float
A mobile you had made, a butterfly,
From a room's high rafter. You are standing on
A stepstool, I'd guess, or your own sturdy table,
Your gowned arms spread like wings above your head.
It's all a work in progress, it seemed to say,
And brought to mind work I'd had underway
So long I was ashamed, its most recent part
A version of a wanderer's song by Goethe
We'd read in Pau beneath the Pyrenees:

The peaks are all
Peaceful.
You feel
Barely a breath
From the treetops:
The birds keep quiet in the copse.
Patience. You
Will soon be peaceful too.

Your short note asked me to recite the end
Of "Little Gidding" at a fête you'd planned—
Predicted—"death permitting," added our quick friend—
In New York. If I'm alive I will, I promised.

7

A neoplasm: something shaped anew.
Art's epitome—or evil twin.
The source of *art* produces *arms* as well
As *harmony*. Enemies reconciled
Abstractly in your later mandalas?
Those bright, neat canvases stylized the struggle
Exposed in work you'd painted earlier.
"Painted"? Ripped out untimely, wrestled forth,
By means of palette knife and palm as much
As sable brush. Those hard, beautiful compositions
So delicately painful that I wanted
You to call one group of them "Eyelashes."
You made them in the store front that we'd rented
In Baghdad, and in the former *chais* near Pau,
Then in the spare room in your Village flat,
Once Cummings's. When I visited,
You blew a hookah's smoke into my ear.
("Djuna, ya still alive?" they said he'd shout
Up to his neighbor when he came home drunk.
Cummings, painter and writer both at once.)
But your smoke signals made no difference.
Patchouli notwithstanding, I could sense
Neither the Black Madonna nor Inanna.
No matter how tight-knit the music's nets
And spells cast by your friends with castanets
And drums, I stayed too soberly alert.

8

First it was just once more O. Henry's birthday,
Our past master of the surprise ending.
Then the slitting (offstage) of the pilots'
Throats like throats of mongrels practiced on.
Morning, September 11, 2001.
One faithful friend surmised you'd chosen *then*
To die (who had endured so long and yet
Seemed ready to go on for weeks at least),
So you could help the other thousands dying
Suddenly, downstage, "make this next transition,"
Those people flying, people trying to fly,
Babel redoubled, twin towers shuddering down
Just blocks from your loved flat on Patchen Place,
All those minds blazing into that nowhere
Always here, now, your last art seeks to figure.

9

Who am I talking to?
                    Yourself, that's who.
You're talking to yourself. With other selves,
Some of them dead.
                    That's who we are these days.

So then let's come directly to the point—
By "string instead of bow," in that old saying—
Though there are many motions tabled here,
Many loose ends that I will have to leave
Along with salted desk to my young wife
And daughter, who can testify that *knife*
And *knot* are two notes in a chord life strikes
At times. They're just the pair to understand
Glamour and *grammar* as one bow's two strings.

The hunter's bow. And why not the rebabist's?

Passion and measure, the two withstand each other,
Like winds and strings, Marsyas and Apollo.

In school you were the one girl who played sax
In the jazz band, the one who would not rhyme
In workshop, who loved loose, "funky lines"—
As long as they were also "sensitive."

So many loose ends left where we still argue.
An argument within, an argument
That's always only waiting to be joined.
Arguere: to shine out, to make clear
And bold as fists of bricks the posters held
Above the crowd that spring up north in Paris
After you had left. *La lutte continue!*

10

These upright, untuned, uptight, tin pun allies,
These splittings of the etym, their nervous noise …
How you would disapprove. Where is the *soul*?
You'd ask. You might as well demand to know
(More riddles, these, to test the furtive hero)
Where past years go. If dance and dancer differ.
When one might tell a handsaw from a hawk.
Or how a raven's like a writing desk.

Tabula rasa. Table of discontents.
Since you saved it, it has been my stable
Negotiating table. My old times table.
I've been its *host*. Which is—or was—to say
I am its *guest*. We've served each other well
And ill. Like spouses. We entertain our ghosts
(Although there's not much table-rapping here)—
You, and our quick dead friend, and some few others,
Who, untranslatable, inimitable,
Are now the words they gave, and thenceforth could
Not keep, yet often kept despite themselves
(Which is another riddle, though scrutable).

So the conundrums roll up with the thunder
The late night news replays from the Flint Hills
Where summer's tornadoes form above your village
Graveyard, its small, mottled monuments,
Sculptures, stone fruit, motley markers, hard words
Weathered, where even as the restive kids
Who study art and drama to escape
Return to make out when the storm has passed,
Passion and patience come to learn their parts.

III

Variations for Three Old Saws

Poetry makes nothing happen.
Makes it happen like nothing else.
Nothing makes nothing happen like poetry.

That is why poets are legislators.
They make nothing happen.
Otherwise it would never.

When nothing does not happen,
We're stuck with everything else
And no space at all for something.

Poetry cannot make anything
Not make one think
Nothing happens all the time

Inside the emptiness we're made of,
Like all we know we do not know.
Everything's mostly nothing

More than whiteness letters
Like these in these lines
Desiderate.

And poetry depends on nothing.
Like a red wheel barrow,
Nothing makes poetry happen.

Post Avant Pastoral

On another anniversary of our invasion of Iraq

On spring's first day, at loose
ends, Amaranth, dangles
aswing, promenaded
under the euonymus
blossoming all at once
with Ahna and Farnoosh.

They colloquized in prose,
lazy, lavender, mazily Asian
as the *art nouveau* liana
twining the lanai outside
the teahouse by the tor
above the swish swash of ocean

about the raveled notions
it aroused: xerophilous
flowers and philosophies,
the gist of Paul's epistle
to the Laodiceans,
Sapphics and phantom rhymes,

and the contrary kinds
of apophenia.
The sense of lengthening
days tinctured with the scent
of the languid clusters led
to monologues they longed

to read and therefore write
by Augusta Ada Byron,
Godden's Sister Ruth,
Jane Digby el Mezrab,
Constance Gore-Booth,
and Waterhouse's Siren.

They touched too on tattoos;
on some of the new groups
(Dido, Dildo, and the Didgeridoos;
The Blackout Dates; The Drupes);
on books, arms, bras,
and the Man—ol' Ezra's

"usual subjects of conversation
between intelligent men"—
and poems whose syntactical
gaps and disarming solecisms
elided lapse of import
and lack of affect alike,

so readers lauding ludic effects
could finesse the future—
the future of futures, tortures,
kids with stumps, surgical
strikes, shark fins, oil
shares spilled, girls sold—

with guilt shown off like gold.

Little Fundamentalist Song

Where did the wind go?
Come back, come between
Us and the foe,
Harsh khamsin.

Where did the wind go?
Come back, come home.
It's time we blow
These fields clean.

Where did the wind go?
Come back, come up.
We want to sow
Hand-picked seeds.

Where did the wind go?
Come back, come through.
We long to grow
Greedy greens.

Where did the wind go?
Come back, come quick.
We need to hoe
Wicked weeds.

Where did the wind go?
Come back, come glean.
We'll get to crow
While they keen.

Where did the wind go?
Come back, come away.
We've learned to stow
Thought and bleed.

Where did the wind go?
Come back, come see.
Here's where we hone
Guillotines.

Where did the wind go?
Come back, come cleave.
We'd die to know
What we mean.

Where did the wind go?
Come back, come in.
It's time we blow
Widdershin.

Wealth (Horace)

1. Odes 2.17: *Cur me querellis exanimas tuis?*

Why torture me to death with your complaints?
Neither the gods nor I would have me fall
　　Before you fall yourself, Maecenas,
　　　　Roof-tree of my life.

If some precocious bolt should shatter you,
Why, how could I, whom you have sheltered, your
　　Alter ego, survive? Since halves,
　　　　We have to go at once.

I took my vow. Whenever you must go,
Then go must I. I, too. We two—together,
　　Closer than twins—will take our journey's
　　　　Final step together.

The Fates concur with Justice's verdict:
No flame-throwing Chimera will ever part
　　Us now, no hundred-handed Gyges
　　　　Rip my limbs from yours.

Regardless whether Libra, or violent
Scorpio, or lambent Capricorn
　　Presided at my birth, we are
　　　　Ourselves a double star.

Famously, Jove saved you from Saturn's wrath.
He fought off Death, falling on sudden wings
　　Towards you, whose dramatic rescue
　　　　Brought the people to

Their feet to call you back for three encores.
And as for me, that falling tree was de-
   flected by Faunus, deputy
      Of Mercury, patron

Of thieves and poets. Remember your own vow:
Build the proper altar, and sacrifice
   The promised hecatomb. Me,
      I'll offer up my lamb.

2. Odes 3.16: *Inclusam Danäen turris äeneä*

Acrisius, Danäe's fearful father—
Whose banal tower of bronze and oaken portal
And trained attack dogs had been meant to keep
His virgin from a midnight lover—

Made Jupiter and Venus jeer and scoff.
They realized that once the god had changed
Himself to gold dust, infiltration
Would simply be unstoppable.

Gold loves to work its way through famous safeguards—
Or, as lightning, to fracture mortised stones.
The Argive's house itself was struck by lucre,
Then rapidly dilapidated.

Likewise Philip's great bribes pried the gates
Of cities open and blew to shards and flinders
Opponents' claims, while money roiled the seas
And snared fierce admirals as well.

As wealth accumulates, anxiety
Mounts too. And greed. I knew what I was doing,
Maecenas, who styled yourself a horseman merely,
When I maintained my own low profile.

In just the measure one abstains, the gods
Bestow their gifts. Unarmed myself, I must
Desert the moneyed ranks to join the poor
Camp of the richly satisfied,

To be a lord of more than one who buys
And hoards the grain—the grain the peasant worked
So hard to cultivate—then stands alone,
A scarecrow, amid fertility.

Pure water from my simple woodland's stream
And crops I can rely on make me more
Comfortable than any potentate
In fecund Africa can be.

Bees from Calabria do not make honey
For me, nor does Bacchus lay away
For me his vintage wines, nor do the Gauls
Card and spin fine wool for me.

Still, I'm far from destitute. And if
I needed more, I'm sure you would comply.
In any case, I think I can increase
By husbandry my modest profits

Beyond the profits of the covetous
Provincial princes. And it's the greediest
Who gleans at last the least. Who asks at first
The minimum is blest the most.

3. Odes 3.24: *Intactis opulentior*

It simply makes no difference, Friend,
      Once Destiny has nailed your flesh and soul
Like common rafters to a king post,
      How opulent the mansion you yourself

Have built on jetties on the landfill
      Shoveled from ruins of some nearby villas,
How grand the view you have secured
      With right of way to public property.

It's better to have been a nomad,
      Or gypsy vendor always on the move,
Or freedman living in the outskirts,
      Or migrant laborer attendant on

The season only, still unmortgaged,
      Content to leave the well-worked premises
To others who will execute
      Faithfully the contracts that were signed.

Such workers take care of their orphans.
      They don't abuse them—nor do their luckier
Or blonder brides emasculate
      Their men or take up unctuous young lovers.

They hand down what their dauntless parents
      Husbanded, with fidelity,
To spouses and to steady friends.
      They know that perfidy amounts to death.

We need someone like one of them
        To end our civic riots, debauchery,
And prejudice, to curb at last
        This idiocy of license upon license.

Someone the future could call justly
        "Father of Cities" on commissioned statues
Might show the rest of us the way,
        The sycophants who cherish otherwise

Morals only when they've died.
        What do recriminations matter if
Sanctions are not enforced? Or laws
        Themselves, absent simple integrity?

My friend, it simply makes no difference
        Whether we exploit the burning tropics,
Or colonize the freezing Arctic,
        Or sail out to the very ends of earth,

If fear of poverty itself
        Impoverish all of us by driving us,
From excess to excess, to shun
        Heartier climes of prudence and of justice.

We must redress our wrongs and prove
        Ourselves to an exultant multitude
By giving up our gold and jewels
        To charity—or dumping them at sea.

We must uproot materialism
        And avarice, which make us do our worst,
If we expect to scourge ourselves
        And discipline our deliquescent spirit.

No privileged child these days can ride
    A horse, he's so afraid of falling off,
Let alone spear a deer or boar.
    Instead he learns at home illicit games

Of chance or plays with balls or hoops,
    Those vestiges of precious Greek amusements.
Meanwhile his father lies, defrauds
    His friends, and piles up in his treasury

Illegal riches for his heir.
    The profits swell up like a pregnancy—
No, a tumor. They grow and grow—
    And must be terminated for our good.

Hija for Emerson's Birthday

I'm honored to shake the hand of a brave Iraqi citizen
who had his hand cut off by Saddam Hussein.
—President George W. Bush, Washington, D. C., 25 May, 2004

"Just ask yourself," we said back in those days,
"Is this world better off without Saddam Hussein?"
Now that's a simple question. Just ask yourself.

It turned up starkly, undeniably
As that left hand inside the trench Marines were digging
At the prison turned "facility."

(That was that week's excavation headline.
Meanwhile, the relics from the tell near Nasiriyah
Had been looted from the National Museum.)

Is our world better off without Saddam
Hussein, who had cut off so many other hands?
Our president himself had grateful thousands

On hand to honor him, give *him* a hand
In DC on the birthday of the Sage of Concord.
In other words, is this world better off

Without those who have made it better off?
If it's a bit of a riddle, really, how to tell,
Each old hand among us will have a hunch.

Is our world better off without Bobby E. Beasely?
Michael Yuri Tarlavsky? Craig W. Cherry?
Yadir G. Reynoso? Joshua I. Bunch?

Let's ask. These names were on the obituary
Page that day in the LA Times. It's archived. Check it.
But what can we tell from a name? Or measly

Hija *for Emerson's Birthday*

Obit? Well, ask yourself. More than a bit
Of *obit* is in the name Tobit, for instance, but
Just what Tobit—praised for his preparation

For righteous burial of Judahites
Who fell in wars against the Northern Kingdom and Assyria,
And blessed with a devoted son who saved him—

What Tobit would now have to do with us,
Not even our extravagant old Emerson
(Though wait! *Emer*? Cuchulain's perfect mate,

Worked hand-in-hand with him, possessor of
The six great gifts of womanhood, from needlework
Through chastity to sweet words and gentle speech)—

Not even Emerson could tell, who spoke
In praise of nature's "rounds," against the divisive "line,"
Its "bounds of good and ill," and for perverse

Return ("Evil will bless, and ice will burn"),
And who would have turned 201
That day in the merry month of Jumaada Awal

When Bush addressed the brave unnamed Baghdadi.
Raymond R. Faulstich, Jr., Kane M. Funk.
(What names people *have*! Stephen I. Yenser!)

What monikers, what handles for our fallen.
Daniel Lee Galvan … Anyway, without *them*, mind you,
We'd still have that butcher Saddam Hussein.

—Wait! *With* them, you mean, we'd still have Saddam?
—Well, it can be perplexing when it's put like *that*.
—Bemusing. Like the sound of one hand clapping.

—Or one hand washing itself. Is our world better
Off without Roberto Abad? *Abad, Roberto*:
What kind of name is that, in any case?

Middle Eastern? And where's the middle *initial*?
To tell him from his father, of course. A typo? For *Bad,
Roberto A.*? "Good is a good doctor, but

Bad is sometimes better" (Emerson).
Or *W*, where Emerson and Bush dovetail.
It seems Roberto got his girlfriend pregnant

In spite of the "Campaign for Children and Families"
Between Iraqi tours in case he didn't come back
From his second, which of course he didn't,

Not for a second, even, to glimpse his son,
Whose name we are not told. *Hussein*, perhaps—or *George.
Or *Herbert. George Herbert*! (Such embranglement!

"I was entangled in a world of strife"!)
Not that we always want "to know what we don't know"
(Donald K. Rumsfeld). We're better off, long run,

If the right hand doesn't know just what
The left has done, right? This world war's better, for sure,
And to make the world's war better too,

Someone had to sacrifice. And ask
Yourself, just who would make the better sacrifice?
(*Make*: what exactly does that mean?)

The ones who wear elaborate tattoos
(Needlework patient, painful, eldritch, intricate,
Wayward as jazz played on the parlor boombox,

Raddled with fractals like our ruined delta),
Obscurely traceable to a secret Inca rite,
Ink indelible as gang connections

That they could nonetheless obliterate
There by the Tigris, on Boulevard Abu Nawas
(Abu Nawas: the Holy Dissolute,

Master of the wine song and of satire,
First Arab poet to applaud Sayiddah Palm),
Who would otherwise have died at home

In drive-bys, done in by their neighbors? Potheads,
Who'd get as high as Bush's daughter and go AWOL
(LOL) at their first chance? The born

Again, who needn't fear their death? The un-
reborn, spirits aborted by their own vile hands?
The Muslim Americans who had their doubts?

 The ones who had no doubts? Just ask yourself.
(And *how many* are we better off without?
Is *this* where quantity turns quality?)

The world is better off without Iraqis
Who are better offed in the right course of things.
Without Hussein's own sons, and theirs, their sons,

We mean, and then which other ones? The Sunnis?
Shias? Some Sunnis and reactionary Shias?
The Ba'athist Sunnis and extremist Shias

Who hate them? Or the Kurds? Which ones, exactly?
The large Kurds? The older, hairy, moldy ones,
That is, whose cheesy lives were mostly lived?

Or the small Kurds, who had no lives or hair.
The cottage Kurds? But not the urban Kurds? The turbaned
Kurds—those darker ones? The whey-faced ones?

The anti-American ones? The Jewish ones?
The anti-Ku-Klux-Klan-and-anti-NRA ones?
The ones who "hate our freedom"—and our baseball?

The atheists? And there are some among them,
Not fit to enter any god's Green Zone, perforce
Denied the houris, halos, hemp, and harps.

Or the Yazidis? Yes, *that* would make some sense,
Since they refuse to wear the colors green and blue,
And since they are so primitive they think,

In the beginning, God made the world a pearl,
And since they are so ancient, weak, impure, muddling
As they do trace elements of Islam,

Christianity, and Mithraism, with some
Oddball Sufism and stray Iranic superstitions.
Are there Iraqi Buddhists? No, really:

Are there? If you can't say, will *they* be missed?
—Well, shame on you, if *that* is not the old epist-
emological enigma wrapped

In a conundrum!—Or a *condomrun*,
As Bush might say on an off day. Just ask yourself:
Is our world better off today? Without

David L. Potter? For whom? The Bushes? And how
About the Potters? Are "his remains" in Arlington?
To Arlington we'll bring our "idle flowers,"

69

Hija *for Emerson's Birthday*

Then—though "Every aster in my hand
Goes loaded with a thought" (Emerson again).
Loaded. And what do we mean by *remains*?

We used to mean: to continue to belong to.
It's doubtful that that definition remains to it.
Is a "left hand" an instance of remains?

And what to make of this morning's "Missing Remains"?
And "Remains Missing"? Years after Bush's off-hand
Remark, new headlines from old headstones spring:

"Thousands of Graves Are Misidentified
Or Unmarked at National Cemetery"—the names
Broken off like handles from their vessels—

Where also mud-caked markers line the banks
Of a purling stream (unnamed) and lie deep in its bed.
"Were they used as riprap to prevent

The stream's erosion?" our good reporter asks.
"Were they engraved incorrectly, hence
Discarded?" *Engraved. Incorrectly. Discarded.*

Is Arlington's our potter's field today?
If so, as Abu Nawas's closest student asked,
"Who is the potter, pray, and who the pot?"

"How gladly with proper words the soldier dies,"
Stevens's line assures us. But on the other hand,
What are the proper words? Is that word proper?

And shouldn't that have been "the soil's erosion"?
Erosion. So how would *Eros* figure here? Just ask
Yourself. Of course he wouldn't! Be rational.

Hija *for Emerson's Birthday*

And so we must mean Cupid. Cupidity
Is one thing we'd associate with "the soil's erosion."
Or should that be "the oil's erosion"? "The soul's"?

Are we better without our soldiers,
Not to mention their daughters, inconceivable,
Who might have married deep-rigged princes' sons

(As Bush's daughters, sweet or crude, must have might
Have done)? Without the so-called martyrs' younger sisters,
Paradisical virgins, immaculately

Pregnant with bombs beneath matte black abayas?
Bush's Baghdadi's daughter's better off, we're sure.
(And he was just a southpaw anyway.)

Or is it the rebellious, the disobedient,
Whose sisters' brothers died on *our* side near Samarra,
Without whom our world's (*mostly*) better off?

It's hard to tell, when they have veils. It's hard
To tell, when phantom limbs will report again tomorrow,
Just whom we're better off without. But ask

Yourself, can we condemn "the vanity
Of false distinctions … " in light of Presidential Scripture?
"If thy right hand offend … " —We must cut Matthew

Off quick as RFK, alas, in order
To go now to commercial. We're sorry. We're in the hands
Of the commercial. We leave you with this question:

Would our world be better off without yourself?
Or your neighbor? —A *little* better, you mean (on balance)?
Who tells us so? What do you mean by *self*?

—Your handy Bible? —And the Milky Way?
Would it be better off without this blue-green pearl of Earth?
But who could tell? But if no one could tell …

What can we mean by *tell*? Now that's a simple question.

Codicil

Wait! To my covert "reader" (who knows who
he is, although he hides his name like sin
from me), I leave all margins blank herein,
that he may prove again his men's room wit,
if once more given his chance to "review"
verses beyond his ken, and show anew
what he can't do—and can, with his short grease pen—
and with the breezy, drizzly ass he blew
in on one nasty dawn, my favorite
easterly editor, whose name I pass
over like wind, to whom I leave, alas,
exactly what he's got. And not. Amen.

IV

Musing

"Here is no penance, much less innocence"

—Donne, "Elegy XIX"

1.

Dear *Melissa*—daughter of
Deborah, Hebrew for *bee*,
From *dbr*, linked to words for *truth* and *word*—
Whose own name glows
Translucently as honey, or the amber
Embalming that famous Baltic bee
Since fifty million years before Alexander
Tried to have his corpse preserved in honey,
Translucently as we say love
Must glow, must glue, must be,
Won't you buzz me?

2.

Because it's all lubricity,
As slickery Emerson puts it.
Sleeping Beauty awake
Is Slipping Booty is *Nudis Verbis*.
Slips of the tongue
Are sips of the truth, or nips,
As your tipsy Thomas didn't doubt.
So, well, the tongue trips
Between lips, skips
To nibbles, leaps slopes,
Lopes, loops Alps,
Slops betwixt,
Stoops to anything,
Sloopsmooth and slaphappy,
To hips, to lap,
And, sapping itself, lapping
Itself, licks slick
The very apsis.
But then the tongue's an asp,
An asp that lapses,
Falls to the facile,
So lisps and limps
(However limpidly)
To sleep at last.

3. (melismatic)

*melissa meliss ah listen to me listen new me a melamed listen a
my list less meli alas than lisztian melos melis alias a lissome lass
lest I be less be lost beeless a mull is a mull is a spicy thought
see thought sigh and see spot spy seathoughts beethoughts with
honey with moon honeymill honeymellow oenomel mell us
melicious melissa*

4.

We need a dash—Dickinsonian?—of censorship—
To cut—to lace—the Yensership.
Let's cut away. Let's have our aches and Keats them too.
We'll bruise the sheets—and then we'll shoot the breeze.

These rudderless vessels in the sea of language,
Shuddering rips in the wake of songwage,
Bees in a blow, only mean I long for you
And make what beelines I can in the way of pleas.

Testy Canticles (Catullan)

1. To Lucy

Come on, Sweetie, *vivamus*, since we vamoose,
Since we decamp, that is, our weedy camp
With such alacrity, however lachrymose,
And in such campy weeds as come to lamp
This dark night of the pigs' long-dreaded knocks.
So come on now, before we bug out, duck
In here with me, where darkling we can buck
Refrains out, so to speak. Our sun's a phoenix,
But since we bounce down these steps once, Pun'kin,
Let's tuck our tokens in and make it all,
From lower Queens up through the Kush of Candace,
From Buddha's Temple of the Tooth in Kandy
Through Cancún's bush to Rangoon, one kingdom come
Cum bang-up subway ride, loot sacks ajangle.

2. For Muse, Her Missing Parakeet

The cat has got your tongue? If so, Cat, tell us,
"There bein' more'n one way t'untie tongues,"
Or so we backward stammered out in Kansas.
Later at Bard it was "there's more than one
Way to scan a kitty." But, Cat with the skinny,
Yours was the Latin jazz whose scat was kin
To our scatback's canny cuts and our sloe gin
Skinny-dips by the river willows' catkins
And tracking scat and reading frosting signs
Through skinflint fields. You had so many lives,
You even turned up purring in the drive-ins
In Wichita in 1959's
Midnights, as Eisenhower's powers passed,
While Lucy conjugated for the class.

At the Bar

1. Akbar

In Silver Lake on Sunset Boulevard at Fountain

Our tumblers clicked, at least. But verse,
she countered, turns: lithe turning's all.
For its part, your prose's stiff hemp rope,
straining to reach around the world,
gets picked to oakum at the end.
That's a mug's game. A convict's rap.
As one old pro's defined their parting,
Prose proceeds, verse reverses.
(Please to hear those trenchant trochees.)
Verse *verts*, in short. So it subverts
inverts, perverts converts. It averts—
and adverts. It is, like it
and not, a matter of advertising,
of turning the mind, indeed the head,
quick as the proverbial tables—
which it's also verdant as.
—Hm? *Gaming* tables. It's vertible,
versatile, will intuit.
Is … *versute*. While prose goes on,
poetry goes down. Gets to it.
Like this iced arak. Goes surely down
to pick us up. It's always ambling
down some dune toward the oasis
even as its subject's clambering
back up a pyramid. Prose flows,
watery. But poetry …
poetry's the acacia tree's
rooting, and shooting, fractally—
a river with its tributaries.
Your "prose poem": it's a sphinx—

monstrous and imaginary.
A poem, conversing with its tropes,
can lead to its own heady problems,
to be sure. Having got there at last,
exhausted, looking down, I thought—
why not?—that I would jump from Cheops'
leveled top. From there, the Nile,
its floodplain's cord of malachite
stretching across that mummy brown
toward the delta, simply *transports*.
One sees forever—with Rilke's "arid
Clarity of a dead man's mind."
So I turned away, sat tight,
took the falafel from my backpack.
One loses one's vertiginy,
as I think Alice put it, bite
by bite. *She smiled. We clicked our tumblers.*

2. Napa Valley Grille

In Westwood on Glendon at Linwood

A good line? It's a point
that *moves*. Its quest's for gist.
For seed and quid. For jot
and tittle's pith and pit.
The rooting reflex. Take *nip*
[*she rapped the table once*],
your word just now for what
we're having. It's a tip
as well, a hill's peak,
its nab or nap. As act,
to nip is to bring together
smartly, to squeeze, to pinch,
and even, surrepti-
tiously [*she winked*], to wink.
Hence *to nip in the bud—bud*:
a small bulge or knob,
a nib, or beak, or neb
containing the organism
(as an ink bead the word)—
is *to snuff the fruit*.

[*She took a sip.*] And yet
to nip this bud's to draw
it out—like our chat, no?—
into its fuller self.
Alerted thus, bestirred,
embodied in the mouthing
(at heart a voiceless plosive)
my point's the thing itself
latches and pulls the object

forth that is its subject,
its lemma, lore, and logic,
pop's pip and matter's nub.

Old Man in a Waterfront Taverna

He labors a text
on a polished marble slab
    whose wrought iron base
(treadle intact) once held up
a sewing machine (Singer).

*

In Beirut *tasbih*,
kombolöi on Thera:
    click by amber click,
worry bead on worry bead,
    koukí tó koukí,
    syllable by same,
while others said their sayings,
his bag filled with beans.

*

From Akrotiri,
high on its desolate hill,
    Oia looks like snow.
It is not snow he knows. Still,
    Oia too will go.

*

The settling sun pools
like metal molten under
    acetylene flame,
    while its rictal mask
defines the moonskull rising.

*

Nursing pellucid raki,
   parsing a hard verse
   as candle flames nod
in two shot glasses, he sips
   some inner light straight.

*

Overlapping with small waves,
   deepening with thought
coming back into its own,
   rocking itself back
awake until he voices
   Cavafy's "*Phonès*,"
shadows that fill the cove fade
   into night they've made.

The Eel (Montale)

The eel, the siren
of freezing seas who flees the Baltic
bound for our seas,
our estuaries, rivers,
who bucks the currents, in the depths,
from branch to branch, then
from capillary to capillary, thinner,
ever more inner, ever nearer the bedrock's
heart, reaching
into torpid pools until one day
sunlight scattered by the chestnut trees
quickens a flickering in muddy puddles,
in freshets that plunge
down Apennine cliffs into Romagna;
the eel, torch, quirt,
Love's earthy dart
our foul ditches or dried-up
Pyrenean brooks alone bring back
to fecund paradises;
green anima who seeks
life there where only
drought and desert gnaw,
scintilla who insists
that all begins when it all seems
buried stump, carbonized;
fleet iris, twin
to what your eyelashes set
to gleam out immaculate from among the sons
of man, sunk in your muck, can you
not call her sister?

Santorini

Mother of Stone, Cybele,
Stone Mother, keep me low,
Resigned, involved, confusable
As to the novice eye the vine
With wild thyme and caper, close
To your chemic soil—
Ash, tuff, and pumice—twined
In on itself to stand
Up under summer wind
And to condense the sure, sheer mist
That plumps until night harvest
Grapes tanged with sulfur, pressed
Then to a salt-tinged must,
Oak barrel ready,
A touch acidic, wit-dry, heady.

Psalm on Sifnos

One does not want,
O Lord, to heap
Up by still waters
Of words a cairn
But hopes to attend
A small covert
Of tamarisk
Whose leaves salty
Yet feathery
Will shed light over
The thickened plot.

One wants at last
To cede the field
To tamarisk
And mastic tree,
To olive and stone,
Stones in the fruit,
Seed in the stones.

A Note About the Author

Stephen Yenser is Distinguished Professor of English Emeritus at the University of California, Los Angeles, and curator of the Hammer Poetry Series at the Hammer Museum. Born in Wichita, Kansas, he took his B.A. from the University of Wichita and his Ph.D. from the University of Wisconsin. His most recent volume of poems is *Blue Guide* (Chicago). *The Fire in All Things* (LSU) received the Walt Whitman Award from the Academy of American Poets. His other honors include the B. F. Connors Prize from the *Paris Review*, an Ingram Merrill Fellowship, a Pushcart Prize, three appearances in the *Best American Poetry* series, two Fulbright Fellowships (one to France and one to Greece), and the Harvey L. Eby Award for the Art of Teaching at UCLA. He has also taught at the University of Baghdad. He has written three critical books (*Circle to Circle: The Poetry of Robert Lowell*; *The Consuming Myth: The Work of James Merrill*; and *A Boundless Field: American Poetry at Large*). He is co-literary executor for James Merrill and co-editor for Merrill's *Collected Poems,* the *Collected Prose*, the *Collected Novels and Plays*, the epic *The Changing Light at Sandover*, and the *Selected Poems*. Merrill's *Selected Letters* is underway.

Other Books from Waywiser